P9-EGK-132

Prehistoric Animals

PREHISTORIC FLYING REPTILES

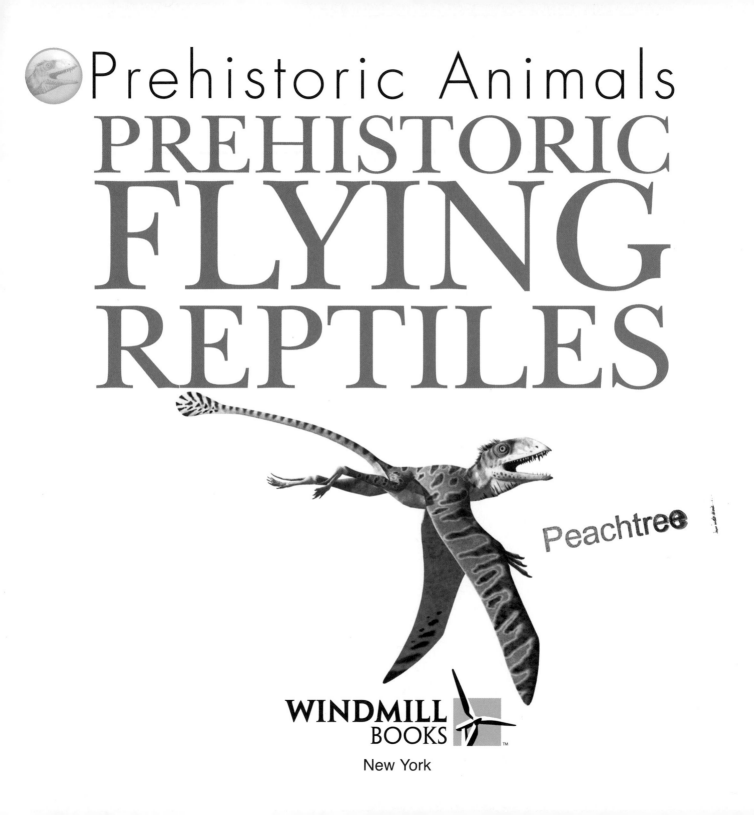

Peachtree

WINDMILL BOOKS

New York

Published in 2016 by **Windmill Books**,
an Imprint of Rosen Publishing
29 East 21st Street, New York, NY 10010

Designed and illustrated *by* David West

Cataloging-in-Publication Data
West, David.
Prehistoric flying reptiles / by David West.
p. cm. — (Prehistoric animals)
Includes index.
ISBN 978-1-5081-9037-0 (pbk.)
ISBN 978-1-5081-9038-7 (6-pack)
ISBN 978-1-5081-9039-4 (library binding)
1. Pterosauria — Juvenile literature. I. West, David, 1956-. II. Title.
QE862.P7 W47 2016
567.918—d23

Manufactured in the United States of America
CPSIA Compliance Information: Batch #BW16PK: For Further Information contact Rosen Publishing, New York, New York at 1-800-237-9932

Contents

Anhanguera

ahn-han-GAIR-ah

Anhanguera was a large flying reptile that lived during the age of the dinosaurs. It fed on fish by flying close to the ocean. Its beak had long, sharp teeth. They were ideal for snatching slippery fish that were swimming just under the sea's surface.

Anhanguera had a wingspan of 15 feet (4.5 m) and weighed around 40–50 pounds (18.1–22.7 kg).

Anhanguera means "Old Devil" in Portuguese.

Anhanguera had very weak legs so it probably spent most of its time in the air.

5

Dimorphodon

die-MORE-foe-don

Dimorphodon was a
medium-sized **pterosaur**
that lived in coastal regions.
It caught fish with its long, spiky
front teeth. Smaller teeth in the back
of its mouth were used to chew its catch.

6

Dimorphodon had a wingspan of 4 feet (1.2 m) and weighed around 5 pounds (2.3 kg).

Some scientists think that *Dimorphodon* may have eaten insects. Its jaw could close very quickly, which was ideal for catching darting insects.

Dimorphodon means "Two-formed Tooth" after the two types of teeth in its mouth.

Dorygnathus means "Spear Jaw."

Dorygnathus
DOOR-rig-NATH-us

Dorygnathus was an older relative of *Dimorphodon*. Its beak was quite different and filled with spear-like teeth. It used these to snag fish.

Scientists think that *Dorygnathus* could walk around on two legs when it wasn't flying.

Dorygnathus had a wingspan of 5 feet (1.5 m) and weighed around 5 pounds (2.3 kg).

Eudimorphodon had a wingspan of 2 feet (0.6 m) and weighed just a few pounds.

Paleontologists have found fossil remains of a fish inside the stomach of a *Eudimorphodon* fossil.

Eudimorphodon means "True Two Types of Tooth."

Eudimorphodon

YOU-die-MORE-fo-don

This flying reptile had a long snout crammed with over one hundred teeth. Some of these teeth were like fangs and ideal for catching fish.

Peteinosaurus

peh-TINE-oh-SAWR-us

Like most flying reptiles, *Peteinosaurus* had very light bones. Unlike most of the previous pterosaurs this little flyer hunted insects such as dragonflies. It had short wings which probably helped it to dart around after fast, flying insects.

Peteinosaurus had a wingspan of 2 feet (0.6 m) and weighed around 4 ounces (0.1 kg).

Peteinosaurus means
"Winged Lizard."

Peteinosaurus, like
many other flying
reptiles, had a long,
stiff tail with a vane
at the end. It used
this to help it steer.

13

Pteranodon

teh-RAN-oh-don

Pteranodon was a large pterosaur that used rising warm air currents to keep flying. It used its long wings to glide over the oceans. It probably caught fish by scooping them from the sea and swallowing them whole, like modern pelicans do.

Pteranodon means "Toothless Wing" because it was a flying reptile with a toothless beak.

Pteranodon had a wingspan of 20 feet (6 m) and weighed around 20–50 pounds (9–22.6 kg).

Pteranodon had a foot-long (30 cm) crest that grew from the back of its head. It may have used this to help steer or as a colorful display to impress female *Pteranodons*.

Pterodactylus

TEH-row-DACK-till-us

Pterodactylus was a small member of
the pterosaur family. Like all the
flying reptiles in this book its wings
were made of thin skin stretched
between its body and its long arm
and finger bones. It probably fed
on fish and flying insects
such as dragonflies.

Crests have only been found on large, adult *Pterodactyluses* so they were probably a form of display.

Pterodactylus had a wingspan of 5 feet (1.5 m) and weighed around 10–20 pounds (4.5–9 kg).

Pterodactylus means "Wing Finger" which refers to the way the wing is supported by one large finger.

Quetzalcoatlus is named after the Aztec god Quetzalcoatl.

Quetzalcoatlus had a wingspan of 50 feet (15.2 m) and weighed around 440–550 pounds (200–250 kg).

Quetzalcoatlus
KWET-zal-co-AT-lus

This was the largest creature ever to take to the skies. *Quetzalcoatlus* probably **scavenged** on the dead bodies of large, long-tailed dinosaurs such as *Alamosaurus*.

Scientists think that this massive creature would have needed a slope to run down in order to take off!

Rhamphorhynchus had a wingspan of 5.9 feet (1.8 m) and weighed up to 11 pounds (5 kg).

A fossil has been discovered of *Rhamphorhynchus* with a fish attached to its wing. It might have been attacked by a large fish as it flew close to the water's surface.

Rhamphorhynchus means "Beak Snout."

Rhamphorhynchus

ram-foe-RINK-us

Rhamphorhynchus was a small flying reptile with a toothy beak.

It probably snatched fish from close to the water's surface. Some scientists think that it may have been active at night like modern-day bats.

Zhejiangopterus

ZHE-zhang-OP-ter-us

Zhejiangopterus was another big pterosaur. It had a long, pointy beak and a long neck.

Zhejiangopterus means "Zhejiang Wing."

It had a wingspan of 12 feet (3.6 m) and weighed around 75 pounds (34 kg).

Zhejiangopterus had long legs and walked on all fours. It might have **preyed on** small animals on the ground, such as lizards.

Glossary

paleontologist
A scientist who studies early forms of life, chiefly by examining fossils.

pterosaur
The name given to the family of flying reptiles that lived during the age of the dinosaurs.

preyed on
Hunted and killed other animals for food.

scavenged
Fed off animals that are already dead.

Timeline

Dinosaurs lived during the Mesozoic Era, which is divided into three main periods.

TRIASSIC	JURASSIC			CRETACEOUS	
Upper	Lower	Middle	Upper	Lower	Upper
230	205	180	159 144	98	65

Millions of Years Ago (mya)